# TEA
## — WITH —
## Mrs BEETON

**TEATIME TREATS**

# TEA

— WITH —

## Mrs BEETON

TEATIME TREATS

WARD LOCK

First published 1990 by Ward Lock
Villiers House, 41/47 Strand, London WC2N 5JE, England

A Cassell imprint

**British Library Cataloguing in Publication Data**
Beeton, Mrs, 1836-1865
  *Tea with Mrs. Beeton.*
  1. Teas – Recipes
  I. Title
  000.00

*ISBN 0-7063-6888-6*

Designed by Cherry Randell
Illustrations by Mike Shoebridge
Edited by Alison Leach and Helen Douglas-Cooper

Typeset in Goudy Old Style by Litho Link Ltd, Welshpool, Powys, Wales

Printed and bound in Italy by Olivotto

# CONTENTS

# $\mathcal{I}$NTRODUCTION

Tea-drinking dates back to 2750 BC in China, but it did not reach England until the mid-seventeenth century. The first tea arrived in Europe by way of Holland and Portugal, as a result of the travels of the colonial fleets of those two countries around Japan and China. It filtered through to Britain via the aristocracy and travelling merchants, and then, in 1662, Charles II married a Portuguese princess, Catharine of Braganza, who happened to be an avid tea-drinker. She brought with her, as part of her dowry, a chest of tea, and she quickly introduced tea-drinking to her friends at court.

However, it took a further hundred years for tea to become the national British beverage. Many people were opposed to tea, saying that it was bad for the nerves. Others said that it was a cure-all, and wrote lengthy broadsheets extolling its virtues. But at this point tea was very expensive

because it was taxed very heavily. This led to smuggling and adulteration with such substances as liquorice leaves, molasses and clay, ash leaves and sheep's dung. Laws to control these practices were introduced in 1725, and the tax was eventually lowered from 119 per cent to 19 per cent. Tea therefore became more accessible, and by the 1750s was the most popular drink in Britain.

The very English ritual of taking afternoon tea is believed to have been invented by Anna, the seventh Duchess of Bedford, in the early nineteenth century. Breakfast in those days was taken at 9 or 10 in the morning, and dinner, which had previously been eaten at 2 or 3 o'clock, was not now eaten until the evening. The Duchess found that she was rather peckish by about 4 o'clock and instructed her maid to bring a tray of tea and some light refreshments to her rooms. She found this arrangement so satisfactory that she started inviting friends to join her, and soon all of London was sipping elegant cups of tea and nibbling dainty sandwiches between 3 and 4 o'clock. As the custom grew, tea-ware rapidly developed from the early earthenware or porcelain cups imported from China to the full tea service that we know today. Chinese teacups had no handles and nor did the first ones made at the English potteries. The idea of the handle was adapted from the 'posset cup', a tall, handled cup in which mulled ales and wines were served. Saucers were deeper than today and at one time it was quite acceptable to drink the tea from it rather than from the cup.

Today the ritual of afternoon tea has made a come-back. Many people are again enjoying the chance to relax in the middle of the afternoon, chat with friends and sip a deliciously refreshing cup of tea.

# TYPES OF TEA

## BLACK, OOLONG AND GREEN TEAS

All tea is picked when two leaves and a bud have formed. The best tea is produced when the tea bush is growing slowly. In high temperatures and times of heavy rainfall the bush grows too quickly and gives weak tea. Different countries and different regions produce different-tasting teas. The flavour depends on the soil, the climate, the altitude, the origins of the bushes, the cultivation methods, the plucking of the leaves and the processing. Different processes produce three different types of tea – black, oolong tea and green tea.

### Black tea

The leaves of black tea are dried after plucking and then machine-rolled and oxidized (fermented) to a bright coppery colour. The leaves are then further dried out in hot-air chambers, during which time they turn black, and the sugars in the tea are caramelized, giving the leaves their familiar, slightly burnt aroma.

### Oolong tea

Oolong tea is processed in the same way as black tea but the fermentation period is much shorter, so the leaves do not become quite as dark. The resulting flavour is mid-way between black tea and green tea.

### Green tea

Green tea is usually picked at the beginning of the season. After plucking, the leaves are steamed to destroy the enzymes that would cause fermentation, then they are rolled and fired, producing grey-green balls. The leaves acquire none of the colour or burnt flavour of black tea, and the resulting liquor is a pale yellow.

## GRADING THE LEAVES

Tea leaves are sorted by leaf size and type. There are four main categories of leaf size:

- leaf tea – mainly large, unbroken leaves
- broken – larger leaf particles that have been broken during the initial process
- fannings – smaller, whole leaves
- dust – broken, smaller leaves (these generally go into tea bags)

Within these leaf categories the tea is further graded according to particular leaf characteristics. The names can be very misleading – Orange Pekoe, for example, is a term referring only to the leaf grade and has nothing at all to do with flavour.

## DIFFERENT TYPES OF TEA

### Indian Teas

*Assam* – a black tea from the Brahmapatra valley, giving a brisk, rich flavour. Serve with milk.

*Darjeeling* – a black tea from the foothills of the Himalayas of West Bengal, giving a light, delicate tea that is known as the champagne of teas. Serve with or without milk and perhaps with a slice of lemon.

*Nilgiri* – a black tea from the Nilgiri Hills of Southern India. It has a light, bright, fairly delicate flavour. Serve with or without milk.

*Ceylon* – black teas from Ceylon give a full flavour and a golden liquor. High-grown Ceylon tea is considered to be one of the best in the world. Serve with milk.

### African teas

*Kenya* – a good all round black tea with a strong flavour and a deep, reddish-gold liquor. Serve with milk.

### China teas

*Keemun* – is the traditional black tea from Imperial China. It has a light delicate flavour and is ideal served with Chinese food. Serve with or without milk.

*Lapsang Souchong* – a black tea from the province of Fujian in the south-east of China. It has a pungent, smoky flavour and is a perfect summer tea. Serve without milk but perhaps with a slice of lemon.

*Jasmine* – an exotic green tea scented with the addition of jasmine flowers. It gives a pale liquor and has a delicate flavour. Serve without milk.

*Gunpowder* – a green tea from the Zhejiang province in the east of China. It has a very delicate flavour and produces a straw-coloured liquor. Serve without milk.

*Rose Pouchong* – an oolong tea from Guangdong in the south east of China, mixed with rose petals and with a very delicate flavour. Serve without milk.

*Formosa/China Oolong* – a large-leafed oolong from the Fujian region in the south-east of China. It has a delicate, almost peachy flavour. Serve black or with a slice of lemon.

*Formosa/China Pouchong* – the leaves of this oolong tea are scented with gardenia, jasmine or yulan blossom, and the liquor is a pale, pinky-brown. Serve black or with a slice of lemon.

### Blended teas

*Earl Grey* – a blend of China teas mixed with citrus oil of bergamot. It has a light, subtle flavour. Serve with or without milk or with a slice of lemon.

*English Breakfast* – a blend of Indian and Ceylon teas with a strong, brisk flavour. Best served with milk.

*Irish Breakfast* – this is usually a blend of Assam teas and has a good, full-bodied flavour. It is best served with milk.

### Scented and flavoured teas

There is an increasing number of scented and flavoured teas on the market today. They are usually made with a blend of black tea mixed with dried fruits or flowers. The most common are apple, blackcurrant, cherry, cinnamon and spice, lemon, lime, mandarin orange, mint, nutmeg and cinnamon, vanilla. They are best drunk without milk.

## TEA AND HEALTH

One cup of tea contains just under 40mg of caffeine (a cup of coffee contains about 80mg). When the tea is drunk the caffeine is released very gradually and helps to stimulate the central nervous system and respiration and therefore fights fatigue and helps heighten alertness. Whereas the caffeine in coffee is released all at once into the system, the full effects of the caffeine in tea are felt about 15 minutes after drinking.

## INFUSIONS AND TISANES

Infusions and tisanes are brewed from the leaves of seeds, fruits, roots, flowers and herbs other than the tea bush, and are sometimes referred to as teas. The name, however, should really only be applied to drinks made from the tea bush (*camellia sinensis*). Infusions are popular today as they contain no caffeine, often have healing properties and are soothing and refreshing. They are best served weak with no milk, and with a slice of lemon and sometimes with sugar or honey. The best known infusions are:

*camomile* – this is said to be good for soothing aches and pains and helps to induce sleep.

*elderflower* – a traditional remedy for gout, this infusion also helps to soothe nerves.

*ginseng* – this is thought to be a cure for impotence.

*limeflower* – a refreshing drink that eases headaches and helps to induce sleep.

*peppermint* – helps digestion and is thought to be good for colds.

*rosehip* – a soothing, delicate drink.

*rosemary* – this is thought to stimulate the memory.

*sage* – good for sore throats.

# $\mathcal{M}$AKING A

## PERFECT CUP OF TEA

### TEA BAGS OR LOOSE TEA?

It is unquestionably true that loose tea leaves give a better cup of tea than tea bags, but some of the bags now available are so good that it has become harder to tell the difference. In the past, the only tea bags in the shops were generally filled with ordinary, everyday quick-brew tea which suits some people but by no means everybody. This type of bag usually contains the smallest particles of tea (dust) that are produced during processing. It gives a quickly-brewed, strong cup of tea, but lacks the finer, subtler flavour of the larger, unbroken leaves. However, the quality and variety of tea bags

has greatly improved. Better quality tea is now used, and bags containing unusual blends, scented and flavoured teas are now readily available. Tea bags do have advantages over loose tea. They are easier to handle and easier to dispose of. If loose tea leaves sit in the tea pot for too long the tea becomes bitter and stewed, but tea bags may be lifted out of the tea pot as soon as the tea has teached the desired strength. Alternatively, place loose tea leaves in an infuser which may be removed in the same way as a tea bag.)

### STORING TEA

When stored carefully, tea bags will keep their flavour for up to six months. Loose tea will last for up to two years. Always keep tea in an air-tight box or tin which should be stored in a cool, dry dark place.

## MAKING A POT OF TEA

* Choose a tea pot that is a suitable size for the occasion, and that is made from glass or any metal other than aluminium or chipped enamel.

* Select a tea to suit your personal taste or that of guests.

* Fill the kettle with fresh, cold water and set it to boil. Oxygen is vital for the successful brewing of the tea, and water in the kettle that has already been boiled will not contain enough oxygen.

* When the water is nearly boiling, warm the tea pot with a little of the water, swill it round and then empty from the pot.

* Put into the pot one good teaspoonful of tea (or one tea bag) per person, plus one for the pot.

* Take the tea pot to the kettle and pour the water on to the tea as it is boiling. If the kettle is taken to the tea pot the water will have gone off the boil by the time it is poured on to the tea.

* Put the lid on the pot and leave to brew. Small-leaved tea will take three to four minutes. Larger leaves will need five to six minutes. All tea stops brewing after seven minutes and after a short time will start to taste bitter.

## ENJOYING THE TEA

Tea tastes best when drunk from china or porcelain. Choose a cup that is about 10cm (4in) in height, about 7.5cm (3in) in diameter at the top and 2.5-3.5cm (1-1½in) at the bottom. In shallow, wide cups, or in stoneware or pottery cups or mugs the tea will quickly become cold and unpleasant to drink. Tea should be drunk piping hot.

To really get the full recuperative, revitalizing effects from a cup of tea, set a tray or a table with a pretty cloth, the tea pot, a jug of hot water, a strainer, a cup and saucer, teaspoon, and milk or lemon, relax and enjoy your tea.

# $\mathcal{B}$READS

*Fruit breads are an ideal addition to afternoon or high tea,
and are delicious served warm from the oven and spread
with butter. The loaves are easy to slice and not too sweet.*

## ALMOND BREAD

*fat for greasing*
*flour for dusting*
*75 g/3 oz almonds*
*250 g/9 oz plain flour*
*20 ml/4 tsp baking powder*
*a pinch of salt*
*2 eggs*
*100 g/4 oz granulated sugar*
*60 ml/4 tbsp oil*
*a few drops almond **or** vanilla essence*
*50 g/2 oz caster sugar*

Grease and flour a baking sheet.
Set the oven at 180°C/350°F/gas 4.

Blanch and skin the almonds,
and chop them coarsely. Sift the
flour, baking powder, and salt
together. Beat the eggs and
granulated sugar lightly together in
a large bowl. Add the oil,
flavouring, flour, and almonds, and
mix to form a dough.

With floured hands, form the
dough into a long roll about 7.5
cm/3 inches wide. Place on the
prepared baking sheet, and bake for
about 30–40 minutes or until
lightly browned. Reduce the heat
to 150°C/300°F/gas 2. Leave the
bread on the baking sheet until
nearly cold, then cut slantways into
slices about 1 cm/½ inch thick.
Sprinkle lightly with the caster
sugar and return to the oven for
about 50-60 minutes, until dry and
lightly browned.

MAKES ABOUT 12 SLICES

## DATE OR RAISIN BREAD

*fat for greasing*
*200 g/7 oz plain flour*
*15 ml/1 tbsp baking powder*
*5 ml/1 tsp salt*
*a pinch of bicarbonate of soda*
*100 g /4 oz dates* **or** *seedless raisins*
*50 g/2 oz walnuts* **or** *almonds, whole*
**or** *chopped*
*25 g/1 oz lard*
*50 g/2 oz black treacle*
*50 g/2 oz dark Barbados sugar*
*150 ml/¼ pint milk*

Line and grease a 20 × 13 × 7.5 cm/8 × 5 × 3 inch loaf tin. Set the oven at 180°C/350°F/gas 4.

Sift the flour, baking powder, salt, and bicarbonate of soda into a large bowl. Chop the fruit and nuts finely if necessary, and add them to the dry ingredients.

Warm the lard, treacle, sugar, and milk together in a saucepan over a low heat. The sugar should dissolve, but do not overheat it. Add the liquid to the dry ingredients, and mix until this becomes a stiff batter.

Pour the mixture into the prepared tin and bake for 1½ hours.

Cool on a wire rack. When cold, wrap in foil, and store for 24 hours.

MAKES ABOUT 12 SLICES

## BANANA BREAD

*fat for greasing*
*3 bananas, mashed*
*50 g/2 oz walnuts, chopped*
*200 g/7 oz self-raising flour*
*5 ml/1 tsp baking powder*
*1.25 ml/¼ tsp bicarbonate of soda*
*100 g/4 oz caster sugar*
*75 g/3 oz soft margarine*
*grated rind of ½ lemon*
*2 eggs*
*50 g/2 oz seedless raisins*

Line and grease a 20 × 13 × 7.5 cm/8 × 5 × 3 inch loaf tin. Set the oven at 180°C/350°F/gas 4.

Mix all the ingredients together in a large bowl and beat for about 3 minutes by hand using a wooden spoon, or for 2 minutes in a mixer, until smooth.

Put the mixture into the prepared loaf tin, and bake for 1 hour 10 minutes or until firm to the touch. Cook on a wire rack.

MAKES ABOUT 12 SLICES

## BARA BRITH

*250 ml/8 fl oz milk*
*5 ml/1 tsp sugar*
*25 g/1 oz fresh yeast*
*75 g/3 oz lard **or** butter*
*450 g/1 lb strong flour*
*50 g/2 oz cut mixed peel*
*150 g/5 oz seedless raisins*
*50 g/2 oz currants*
*75 g/3 oz soft brown sugar*
*5 ml/1 tsp mixed spice*
*a pinch of salt*
*1 egg*
*oil for greasing*
*flour for dusting*
*clear honey for glazing*

Warm the milk to 30–35°C/85–95°F with the sugar. Blend the fresh yeast into the milk, and put to one side for 10–20 minutes until frothy.

Rub the lard or butter into the flour until the mixture resembles fine breadcrumbs. Stir in the peel, raisins, currants, brown sugar, mixed spice, and salt. Beat the egg until liquid. Make a well in the centre of the dry ingredients and add the yeast mixture and the beaten egg.

Mix to a soft dough, place in a large, lightly oiled polythene bag, and leave in a warm place for about 2 hours until the dough has doubled in size.

Grease a 20 × 13 × 7.5 cm/8 × 5 × 3 inch loaf tin.

Turn the dough out on to a floured board and knead well. Put it into the prepared loaf tin, pressing it well into the corners. Return to the polythene bag, and leave to rise for a further 30 minutes.

Set the oven at 200°C/400°F/gas 6.

Remove the loaf tin from the bag and bake for 15 minutes. Reduce the temperature to 160°C/325°F/gas 3, and bake for about 1¼ hours. Turn out on to a wire rack, and brush the top of the loaf with clear warm honey while still warm.

Serve sliced, spread with butter.

MAKES ABOUT 12 SLICES

## CHOOSING A TEA POT

It is useful to have several different sizes of tea pot for different occasions – for days when you want to sit peacefully, enjoying a refreshing pot on your own, and for days when all the family or several friends are together for tea. When buying pots it is useful to bear the following guidelines in mind:

*⁎* Choose any material except aluminium or anamel. Aluminium gives the tea a blueish tinge and when enamel becomes chipped it will affect the flavour of the tea.

*⁎* Check that the glaze inside the pot is not cracked or crazed.

*⁎* Check that the handle is easy to grip and leaves plenty of room for the knuckles. If not you will burn your fingers every time you try to pour the tea.

*⁎* There should be a hole in the lid to allow air to pass into the pot as tea is poured out. Without this intake of air, the spout will dribble and make a dreadful mess.

*⁎* There should also be a lug on the lid to hold it in place. Without this there is a strong risk of the lid crashing into the cups as the tea is poured.

*⁎* There should be a strainer at the base of the spout inside the pot to catch the tea leaves as the tea is poured.

### Caring for your tea pot
Do not use detergent inside a tea pot as this will affect the taste of the tea. Remove tannin stains by soaking the pot for several hours with a solution of hot water and 60 ml/4 tbsp of bicarbonate of soda. Rinse well before using.

# SCONES

*A traditional cream tea should include light, freshly made
scones served with preserves and clotted cream. This is
made by heating and skimming the rich, creamy milk of
Dorset, Devon and Cornwall, and is irresistible topped
with a generous dollop of strawberry jam.*

## PLAIN SCONES

*200 g/7 oz plain flour
1.25 ml/¼ tsp salt
50 g/2 oz butter* **or** *margarine*
**and** *one of the following raising
agents:
5 ml/1 tsp bicarbonate of soda
10 ml/2 tsp cream of tartar
125 ml/4½ fl oz fresh milk*
**or**
*20 ml/4 tsp baking powder
125 ml/4½ fl oz fresh milk*

**or**
*5 ml/1 tsp bicarbonate of soda
5 ml/1 tsp cream of tartar
125 ml/4½ fl oz soured milk* **or**
*buttermilk*
**and**
*flour for rolling out
fat for greasing
milk* **or** *beaten egg for glazing
(optional)*

Grease a baking sheet. Set the oven at 220°C/425°F/gas 7.

Sift together the flour and salt into a large bowl. Rub the fat into the flour until the mixture resembles fine breadcrumbs. Sift in the dry raising agents and mix well. Add the milk and mix lightly and quickly to form a soft, slightly sticky dough. Knead very lightly until smooth.

Roll out the dough on a floured surface to about 2.5 cm/1 inch thickness and cut into rounds, using a 5 cm/2 inch cutter. Re-roll the trimmings, and re-cut.

Place the scones on the prepared sheet and brush the tops with milk or beaten egg, if liked. Bake for 7–10 minutes until well risen and golden brown. Cool on a wire rack so that the scones are crisp outside.

For rich scones, add 25 g/1 oz white sugar to the mixed dry ingredients for the basic recipe; instead of mixing with milk alone, use 1 beaten egg with enough milk to make 125 ml/4½ fl oz.

For fruit scones, add 50 g/2 oz caster sugar and 50 g/2 oz currants, sultanas or other dried fruit to the basic recipe.

MAKES 10–12

## DROP SCONES

*200 g/7 oz plain flour*
*5 ml/1 tsp salt*
*25 g/1 oz caster sugar*
*10 ml/2 tsp cream of tartar*
*5 ml/1 tsp bicarbonate of soda*
*1 egg, beaten*
*175 ml/6 fl oz milk*
*fat for greasing*

Lightly grease a griddle or a very thick frying pan. Set over gentle heat until a faint blue haze rises. If the griddle or pan is too hot, the scones brown on the outside before being cooked in the centre.

Sift together the dry ingredients in a mixing bowl three times. Add the egg and milk gradually and mix to a smooth thick batter.

Drop about 10 ml/2 tsp of the mixture on to the griddle or pan. Tiny bubbles will appear and when these burst, turn the scones over, using a palette knife.

Cook the underside until golden brown; then wrap the scones in a clean tea-towel and cool on a wire rack. The scones will take about 3 minutes to cook on the first side and about 2 minutes after turning.

MAKES ABOUT 24

## CRUMPETS

*200 g/7 oz strong flour*
*2.5 ml/½ tsp salt*
*2.5 ml/½ tsp sugar*
*100 ml/4 fl oz milk*
*100 ml/4 fl oz water*
*15 g/½ oz fresh yeast* **or**
*10 ml/2 tsp dried yeast*
*a pinch of bicarbonate of soda*
*15 ml/1 tbsp warm water*
*fat for frying*

Sift together the flour, salt, and sugar into a large bowl. Warm the milk and water in a saucepan until hand-hot. Blend the fresh yeast into the liquid or reconstitute the dried yeast. Add the yeast liquid to the flour and beat to a smooth batter. Cover with a large, lightly oiled polythene bag and leave in a warm place for about 45 minutes or until the dough has doubled in size.

Dissolve the bicarbonate of soda in the 15 ml/1 tbsp warm water and beat into the batter mixture. Cover with the polythene bag and leave to rise again for 20 minutes.

Grease a griddle or thick frying pan and heat until a bread cube browns in 15 seconds. Grease metal rings, poaching rings or large plain biscuit cutters, about 7.5 cm/3

inches in diameter. Place the rings on the hot griddle.

Pour about 15 ml/1 tbsp of batter into each ring so that the batter is about 3 mm/⅛ inch deep. Cook until the top is set and the bubbles have burst. Remove the ring and turn the crumpet over. Cook the other side for 2–3 minutes only until firm but barely coloured. Crumpets should be pale on top. Repeat until all the batter has been used up.

Serve toasted, hot, with butter.

MAKES 10–12

## MUFFINS

*400 g/14 oz strong flour*
*5 ml/1 tsp salt*
*25 g/1 oz butter* **or** *margarine*
*200 ml/7 fl oz milk*
*15 g/½ oz fresh yeast* **or**
*10 ml/2 tsp dried yeast*
*1 egg*
*flour for rolling out*
*fat for frying*

Sift together the flour and salt into a large bowl. Rub in the fat. Warm the milk until hand-hot. Blend the fresh yeast into the milk or reconstitute the dried yeast. Beat the egg into the yeast liquid. Stir the liquid into the flour to make a very soft dough.

Beat the dough with your hand or a wooden spoon for about 5 minutes or until smooth and shiny. Put the bowl in a large, lightly oiled polythene bag and leave in a warm place for 1–2 hours, or until the dough has almost doubled in size. Beat again lightly.

Roll out on a well floured surface to 1 cm/½ inch thickness. Using a plain 7.5 cm/3 inch cutter, cut the dough into rounds. Place the rounds on a floured baking sheet, cover with polythene, and leave to rise at room temperature for about 45 minutes or until puffy.

Lightly grease a griddle or heavy frying pan and heat until a bread cube browns in 15 seconds. Cook the muffins on both sides for about 8 minutes until golden brown.

To serve, split open each muffin around the edges almost to the centre. Toast slowly on both outer sides so that the heat penetrates to the centre of the muffin. Pull apart, butter thickly, put together again, and serve hot.

MAKES 20

◇◇◇◇◇◇◇◇◇◇◇◇◇◇◇◇◇◇◇◇◇◇◇◇◇◇◇◇◇◇◇◇◇◇◇◇◇◇◇◇

## MUFFINS

Muffins were eaten for breakfast and tea in Victorian days and they suit both meals equally well. Mrs Beeton remarked in her *Dictionary of Everyday Cookery* that it was more usual to buy muffins ready prepared than to bake them at home. They were readily available, as the muffin man hawked his wares around the streets every day, carrying his goods on a large tray on his head and ringing his bell to advise people of his approach. For those who made them at home, the dough had to be made in advance and left to rise. The dough for the breakfast muffins was usually made late the previous evening and left in a cupboard above the stove. In the morning they just had to be popped into the stove and baked to a light golden colour.

◇◇◇◇◇◇◇◇◇◇◇◇◇◇◇◇◇◇◇◇◇◇◇◇◇◇◇◇◇◇◇◇◇◇◇◇◇◇◇◇

# CAKES

*The tea table is not complete without at least one large cake, set grandly on a cake stand or plate as the centre of an arrangement of delicious treats.*

❖❖❖❖❖❖❖❖❖❖❖❖❖❖❖❖❖❖❖❖❖❖❖❖❖❖❖❖❖❖❖

## VICTORIAN CAKES
## AND BISCUITS

Home baking in Victorian households varied according to the type of cooking-range in the kitchen. Where an open fire was used biscuits and flat cakes were baked either on a bakestone or griddle that was heated on the fire; or the iron pot in which all the family cooking was done was detached from its hook and turned upside down over a heated stone. In some kitchens with an open range a dome-shaped bread oven was built into the chimney, and this was used once a week to bake the family's supply of bread, pastries and cakes. The oven was heated by a fire of brushwood or faggots and the embers were well spread around to ensure an even heat. The ashes were then scraped out and the bread was put in. Once the bread was baked the residual heat of the oven was used to bake the cakes. In kitchens that were equipped with a closed range, baking was more of an everyday event since the central fire, that was always alight, heated the side ovens and made baking an easier task. The oven temperature was controlled by a system of flues and dampers, but the heat inside was by no means as predictable as in modern ovens. Although commercially-produced cakes had begun to appear in the 1840s and 1850s, most cooks still preferred to bake their own.

❖❖❖❖❖❖❖❖❖❖❖❖❖❖❖❖❖❖❖❖❖❖❖❖❖❖❖❖❖❖❖

## VICTORIA SANDWICH CAKE

*fat for greasing*
*150 g/5 oz butter or margarine*
*150 g/5 oz caster sugar*
*3 eggs, beaten*
*150 g/5 oz self-raising flour or plain*
*flour and 5 ml/1 tsp baking powder*
*pinch of salt*
*raspberry or other jam for filling*
*caster sugar for dredging*

Line and grease two 18 cm/7 inch sandwich tins. Set the oven at 180°C/350°F/gas 4.

In a mixing bowl cream the butter or margarine with the sugar until light and fluffy. Add the eggs gradually, beating well after each addition. Sift the flour, salt and baking powder, if used, into a bowl. Stir into the creamed mixture, lightly but thoroughly, until evenly mixed.

Divide between the tins and bake for 25–30 minutes. Cool on a wire rack, then sandwich together with jam. Sprinkle the top with caster sugar or spread with glacé icing.

MAKES ONE
18 cm/7 inch CAKE

## DATE AND WALNUT CAKE

*fat for greasing*
*200 g/7 oz self-raising flour or 200 g/*
*7 oz plain flour and 10 ml/2 tsp baking*
*powder*
*pinch of grated nutmeg*
*75 g/3 oz margarine*
*75 g/3 oz dates, stoned and chopped*
*25 g/1 oz walnuts, chopped*
*75 g/3 oz soft light brown sugar*
*2 small eggs*
*about 125 ml/4½ fl oz milk*

Line and grease a 15 cm/6 inch tin. Set the oven at 180°C/350°F/gas 4.

Mix the flour and nutmeg in a mixing bowl, and rub in the margarine until the mixture resembles fine breadcrumbs. Add the dates and walnuts with the sugar and baking powder, if used.

In a bowl, beat the eggs with the milk and stir into the dry ingredients. Mix well.

Spoon the mixture into the cake tin and bake for 1¼–1½ hours or until cooked through and firm to the touch. Cool on a wire rack.

MAKES ONE
15 cm/6 inch CAKE

## FESTIVAL FRUIT CAKE

*fat for greasing*
*200 g/7 oz plain flour*
*1.25 ml/¼ tsp salt*
*2.5 ml/½ tsp baking powder*
*50 g/2 oz currants*
*50 g/2 oz sultanas*
*50 g/2 oz glacé cherries, chopped*
*50 g/2 oz cut mixed peel*
*150 g/5 oz butter* **or** *margarine*
*150 g/5 oz caster sugar*
*4 eggs*
*15 ml/1 tbsp milk (optional)*

Line and grease an 18 cm/7 inch cake tin. Set the oven at 180°C/350°F/gas 4.

Sift the flour, salt and baking powder into a bowl. Stir in the dried fruit and mixed peel and mix well. Set aside.

Place the butter or margarine in a mixing bowl and beat until very soft. Add the sugar and cream together until light and fluffy. Add the beaten eggs gradually, beating well after each addition. If the mixture shows signs of curdling, add a little of the flour mixture.

Fold in the dry ingredients lightly but thoroughly, adding the milk if too stiff.

Spoon into the prepared tin, smooth the surface and make a hollow in the centre. Bake for 30 minutes, then reduce the oven temperature to 160°C/325°F/gas 3 and bake for 40 minutes more until firm to the touch. Leave to cool on a wire rack.

MAKES ONE
18 cm/7 inch CAKE

## DUNDEE CAKE

*fat for greasing*
*200 g/7 oz plain flour*
*2.5 ml/½ tsp baking powder*
*1.25 ml/¼ tsp salt*
*150 g/5 oz butter*
*150 g/5 oz caster sugar*
*4 eggs, beaten*
*100 g/4 oz glacé cherries, quartered*
*150 g/5 oz currants*
*150 g/5 oz sultanas*
*100 g/4 oz seedless raisins*
*50 g/2 oz cut mixed peel*
*50 g/2 oz ground almonds*
*grated rind of 1 lemon*
*50 g/2 oz blanched split almonds*

Line and grease an 18 cm/7 inch round cake tin. Set the oven at 180°C/350°F/gas 4.

Sift the flour, baking powder and

salt into a bowl. In a mixing bowl, cream the butter and sugar together well, and beat in the eggs. Fold the flour mixture, cherries, dried fruit, peel and ground almonds into the creamed mixture. Add the lemon rind and mix well.

Spoon into the prepared tin and make a slight hollow in the centre. Bake for 20 minutes, by which time the hollow should have filled in. Arrange the split almonds on top.

Return the cake to the oven, bake for a further 40–50 minutes, then reduce the temperature to 160°C/325°F/gas 3 and bake for another hour. Cool on a wire rack.

MAKES ONE
18 cm/7 inch CAKE

## SWISS ROLL

*fat for greasing*
*3 eggs*
*75 g/3 oz caster sugar*
*75 g/3 oz plain flour*
*2.5 ml/½ tsp baking powder*
*pinch of salt*
*about 60 ml/4 tbsp jam for filling*
*caster sugar for dusting*

Line and grease a 30 × 20 cm/12 × 8 inch Swiss roll tin. Set the oven at 220°C/425°F/gas 7.

Combine the eggs and sugar in a heatproof bowl. Set the bowl over a pan of hot water, taking care that the bottom of the bowl does not touch the water. Whisk for 10–15 minutes until thick and creamy, then remove from the pan and continue whisking until the mixture is cold.

Sift the flour, baking powder and salt into a bowl, then lightly fold into the egg mixture. Pour into the prepared tin and bake for 10 minutes. Meanwhile warm the jam in a small saucepan.

When the cake is cooked, turn it on to a large sheet of greaseproof paper dusted with caster sugar. Peel off the lining paper. Trim off any crisp edges. Spread the cake with the warmed jam and roll up tightly from one long side. Dredge with caster sugar and place on a wire rack, with the join underneath, until completely cool.

MAKES ONE
30 cm/12 inch SWISS ROLL

## MARBLE CAKE

*fat for greasing*
*175 g/6 oz butter* **or** *margarine*
*175 g/6 oz caster sugar*
*3 eggs, beaten*
*few drops of vanilla essence*
*225 g/8 oz self-raising flour*
*pinch of salt*
*30 ml/2 tbsp milk*
*30 ml/2 tbsp strong black coffee*
*50 g/2 oz chocolate, broken into*
*chunks*
*chocolate buttercream*
*15 ml/1 tbsp grated chocolate*

Line and grease a 20 cm/8 inch round cake tin. Set the oven at 180°C/350°F/gas 4.

In a mixing bowl cream the butter or margarine with the sugar until light and fluffy. Add the eggs gradually, beating well after each addition. Stir in the vanilla.

Sift the flour and salt into a bowl. Stir into the creamed mixture, lightly but thoroughly, until evenly mixed. Place half the mixture in a second bowl and beat in the milk.

Combine the coffee and chocolate in a bowl set over a saucepan of simmering water. Heat gently until the chocolate melts.

Stir thoroughly, then add to the cake mixture in the mixing bowl, beating well.

Put alternate spoonfuls of plain and chocolate mixture into the prepared cake tin. Bake for 45 minutes–1 hour, until firm to the touch. Cool on a wire rack. Top with the buttercream and grated chocolate.

MAKES ONE
20 cm/8 inch CAKE

### HIGH TEA

*Welsh rarebit*
*egg and bacon pie*
*bread and butter*
*cheese and pickles*

*Plum bread*
*Old English cider cake*
*basic buns*
*flapjacks*
*brownies*
*Assam*
*Ceylon*
*fruit juice*

## OLD ENGLISH CIDER CAKE

*fat for greasing*
*225 g/8 oz plain flour*
*7.5 ml/1½ tsp grated nutmeg*
*1.25 ml/¼ tsp ground cinnamon*
*5 ml/1 tsp baking powder*
*pinch of salt*
*100 g/4 oz butter **or** margarine*
*100 g/4 oz caster sugar*
*2 eggs*
*125 ml/4½ fl oz dry still cider*

Line and lightly grease a shallow 20 cm/8 inch square cake tin. Set the oven at 180°C/350°F/gas 4.

Sift the flour into a bowl with the spices, baking powder and salt. Cream the butter or margarine with the sugar until light and fluffy, then beat in the eggs. Beat half the flour mixture into the creamed mixture. Beat in half the cider. Repeat, using the remaining flour and cider.

Spoon the mixture into the prepared tin and bake for 50–55 minutes until the cake is cooked through and firm to the touch. Cool on a wire rack.

MAKES ONE
20 cm/8 inch CAKE

## RICH GINGERBREAD

*fat for greasing*
*225 g/8 oz plain flour*
*1.25 ml/¼ tsp salt*
*10 ml/2 tsp ground ginger*
*2.5–5 ml/½–1 tsp ground cinnamon*
***or** grated nutmeg*
*5 ml/1 tsp bicarbonate of soda*
*100 g/4 oz butter*
*100 g/4 oz soft light brown sugar*
*100 g/4 oz golden syrup*
*1 egg*
*45 ml/3 tbsp plain yoghurt*
*30 ml/2 tbsp ginger preserve*

Line and grease a 23 cm/9 inch square tin. Set the oven at 160°C/325°F/gas 3.

Sift the flour, salt, spices and bicarbonate of soda into a mixing bowl. Heat the butter, sugar and syrup in a saucepan until the butter has melted.

In a bowl, beat the egg and yogurt together. Add to the dry ingredients, with the melted mixture, to give a soft, dropping consistency. Stir in the preserve.

Spoon into the prepared tin and bake for 50–60 minutes until cooked through and firm to the touch. Cool on a wire rack.

MAKES 1 × 23 cm/9 inch CAKE

## ROCK CAKES

*fat for greasing*
*200 g/7 oz self-raising flour*
*1.25 ml/¹⁄₄ tsp salt*
*1.25 ml/¹⁄₄ tsp grated nutmeg*
*75 g/3 oz margarine*
*75 g/3 oz sugar*
*75 g/3 oz mixed dried fruit (currants,*
*sultanas, mixed peel, glacé cherries)*
*1 egg*
*milk (see method)*

Thoroughly grease 2 baking sheets.
Set the oven at 200°C/400°F/gas 6.

Sift the flour and salt into a
mixing bowl. Add the nutmeg. Rub
in the margarine until the mixture
resembles fine breadcrumbs. Stir in
the sugar and dried fruit.

Put the egg into a measuring jug
and add enough milk to make up
to 125 ml/4½ fl oz. Add the liquid
to the dry ingredients and mix with
a fork to a sticky stiff mixture.

Divide the mixture into 12–14
portions. Form into rocky heaps on
the prepared baking sheets,
allowing about 2 cm/¾ inch
between each for spreading. Bake
for 15–20 minutes. Cool on a wire
rack.

MAKES 12–14

## CHICAGO CHOCOLATE CAKE

*fat for greasing*
*flour for dusting*
*200 g/7 oz plain flour*
*300 g/11 oz caster sugar*
*50 g/2 oz cocoa*
*10 ml/2 tsp bicarbonate of soda*
*2.5–5 ml/¹⁄₂–1 tsp salt*
*100 g/4 oz soft margarine*
*200 ml/7 fl oz milk*
*2 eggs*
*5 ml/1 tsp vanilla essence*

Filling
*chocolate buttercream*
*chocolate slivers*

Line and grease two 20 cm/8 inch
sandwich tins or a 33 × 23 × 5 cm/
13 × 9 × 2 inch tin. Dust the
lining paper with flour mixed with
a little cocoa to prevent any white
flour residue on the baked cake,
shaking out the excess. Set the
oven at 180°C/350°F/gas 4.

Sift all the dry ingredients into a
mixing bowl. Add the margarine
and 175 ml/6 fl oz of the milk. Stir,
then beat well until smooth,
allowing 2 minutes by hand or
1–1½ minutes with an electric
mixer. Add the remaining milk,

the eggs and essence, and beat for 1 more minute.

Spoon into the prepared tin or tins and bake for 35–40 minutes if using two tins, or 40–45 minutes if using a single oblong tin. When cooked, the cakes should be firm to the touch. Leave to cool until firm before turning out on to a wire rack to cool completely.

When cold, split the oblong cake into two layers crossways, brushing off excess crumbs. Sandwich together with buttercream. Sandwich the layer cake in the same way. Swirl buttercream on top of the cake and add chocolate slivers.

MAKES ONE
20 cm/8 inch ROUND CAKE
OR ONE TRIANGULAR
CAKE

## COFFEE GLACÉ ICING

*about 30 ml/2 tbsp water*
*150 g/5 oz icing sugar, sifted*
*7.5 ml/1½ tsp instant coffee*
*2.5 ml/½ tsp strained lemon* **or**
*orange juice (optional)*

Put 20 ml/4 tsp water into a small non-stick or enamel saucepan with the icing sugar. If a mild lemon or orange flavour is required add the juice at this stage. Warm very gently, without making the pan too hot to touch on the underside. Beat well with a wooden spoon. The icing should coat the back of the spoon thickly. If it is too thick, add the extra water; if too thin add a very little extra sifted icing sugar. Use at once.

# ℬUNS

*Serve a selection of small cakes and buns at any type of tea party. They will suit guests who are content to nibble something dainty and light with their tea, and children love to see lots of small goodies on the tea table.*

## BUTTERFLY CAKES

*fat for greasing*
*100 g/4 oz self-raising flour*
*pinch of salt*
*100 g/4 oz butter* **or** *margarine*
*100 g/4 oz caster sugar*
*2 eggs, beaten*

Decoration
*150 ml/5 fl oz double cream*
*5 ml/1 tsp caster sugar*
*1.25 ml/¼ tsp vanilla essence*
*icing sugar for dusting*

Grease 12–14 bun tins. Set the oven at 180°C/350°F/gas 4.

Mix the flour and salt in a bowl. In a mixing bowl, cream the butter or margarine with the sugar until light and fluffy. Beat in the eggs, then lightly stir in the flour and salt. Divide the mixture evenly between the prepared bun tins, and bake for 15–20 minutes until golden brown. Cool on a wire rack.

In a bowl, whip the cream with the caster sugar and vanilla essence until stiff. Transfer to a piping bag fitted with a large star nozzle.

When the cakes are cold, cut a round off the top of each. Cut each round in half to create two 'butterfly wings'. Pipe a star of cream on each cake, then add the 'wings', placing them cut side down, and slightly apart. Dust with icing sugar.

MAKES 12–14

## CORKERS

fat for greasing
100 g/4 oz self-raising flour
pinch of salt
100 g/4 oz butter **or** margarine
100 g/4 oz caster sugar
2 eggs, beaten

Decoration
apricot glaze
15 g/½ oz pistachio nuts, blanched
and chopped
150 ml/5 fl oz double cream
icing sugar for dusting

Grease 12–14 bun tins. Set the oven at 180°C/350°/gas 4. Mix the flour and salt in a bowl.

In a mixing bowl, cream the butter or margarine with the sugar until light and fluffy. Beat in the eggs, then lightly stir in the flour and salt. Divide the mixture evenly between the prepared bun tins, and bake for 15–20 minutes until golden brown. Cool on a wire rack.

When the cakes are cold, remove a small cylindrical section about 1–2 cm/½–¾ inch deep from the centre of each cake, using an apple corer or small cutter. Have both the apricot glaze and the chopped nuts ready.

Dip the top of each cake cork in glaze, then in nuts. Spoon the rest of the glaze into the hollows in each cake.

In a bowl, whip the cream until stiff. Using a piping bag fitted with a star nozzle, pipe a cream star on top of the glaze in each cake hollow. Return the corks, pressing them down lightly, then dust with icing sugar.

MAKES 12–14

### CHILDREN'S TEA PARTY

a selection of sandwiches
with the following fillings:
peanut butter and grated
cheddar cheese
egg mayonnaise

cold sliced sausage and
tomato ketchup
banana and grated chocolate

sausage rolls

swiss roll
chicago chocolate cake
jam tarts
chocolate chip cookies

milk shakes

## CREAM ECLAIRS

*1 quantity Choux Pastry*
*fat for greasing*
*250 ml/8 fl oz whipping cream*
*25 g/1 oz caster sugar and icing sugar,*
*mixed*
*3–4 drops vanilla essence*
*1 quantity chocolate glacé icing*
*(page 33)*

Set the oven at 220°C/425°F/gas 7.
Lightly grease a baking sheet.

Make the pastry and use it while
still warm. Put it in a forcing bag
with a 2.5 cm/1 inch nozzle, and
pipe the mixture in 10 cm/4 inch
lengths on to the prepared baking
sheet. Cut off each length with a
knife or scissors dipped in hot
water for ease of cutting.

Bake for 30 minutes. Do not
open the oven door while baking.
Reduce the temperature to 180°C/
350°F/gas 4, and bake for a further
10 minutes. Remove the éclairs
from the oven, split them
lengthways, and remove any
uncooked paste. Return to the
oven for 5 minutes if still damp
inside. Cool completely on a wire
rack.

Meanwhile, whip the cream
until it holds its shape, adding the
mixed sugars gradually. Add the
vanilla essence while whipping. Fill
the éclairs with the cream, close
neatly, and cover the tops with
glacé icing.

MAKES 10–12

## CHOUX PASTRY

*100 g/4 oz plain flour*
*250 ml/8 fl oz water*
*50 g/2 oz butter **or** margarine*
*a pinch of salt*
*1 egg yolk*
*2 eggs*

Sift the flour into a bowl. Put the
water, fat and salt in a saucepan,
and bring to the boil. Remove from
the heat and add the flour all at
once. Return to the heat and beat
well with a wooden spoon until the
mixture forms a smooth paste
leaving the sides of the pan clean.

Remove from the heat and cool
slightly. Add the egg yolk, and beat
well. Add the other eggs, one at a
time, beating thoroughly between
each addition. Use as required.

MAKES ABOUT 450 g/1 lb

## CHOCOLATE GLACÉ ICING

*100 g/4 oz plain chocolate*
*20 ml/4 tsp butter*
*30 ml/2 tbsp water*
*150 g/5 oz icing sugar*

Break up the chocolate and put it into a heatproof basin. Stand the basin in a saucepan containing enough hot water to come half-way up its sides. Add the butter and water to the chocolate. Stir over gentle heat until the chocolate and butter melt and become a smooth cream.

Cool slightly, then sift in the icing sugar, and beat until the icing is the consistency for easy spreading. Add a few drops of water if it is too thick; it should coat the back of a spoon. Use at once.

◇◇◇◇◇◇◇◇◇◇◇◇◇◇◇◇◇◇◇◇◇◇◇◇◇◇◇◇◇◇◇◇

## TEA DANCES

Tea dances had been popular in several resorts of the French Riviera for a number of years before the fashion arrived in London in 1912. The craze co-incided with the introduction of the Tango, which had originated in a rather disreputable suburb of Buenos Aires, and had travelled via smart cafés and amateur dance shows to Paris. It quickly became an acceptable and very fashionable ballroom dance, and seems to have made an appearance in London in 1911. At first, people danced between the tables in restaurants and tea rooms, until the Savoy Hotel had the idea of clearing part of the tea room floor to make space for the dancers. Other hotels and even theatres followed suit, and by 1913 tea and tango dances were all the rage, both in London and in the provinces. Dance teachers and the hotels and restaurants that ran tango clubs and regular tea dances made a fortune. People would arrive between 4 and 5 o'clock and dance feverishly for two hours or so, on nothing but a cup of tea and perhaps a few sandwiches, then they would dash away home to change for dinner and more enthusiastic dancing.

◇◇◇◇◇◇◇◇◇◇◇◇◇◇◇◇◇◇◇◇◇◇◇◇◇◇◇◇◇◇◇◇

## FLORENTINES

*oil for greasing*
*25 g/1 oz glacé cherries, chopped*
*100 g/4 oz cut mixed peel, finely*
*chopped*
*50 g/2 oz flaked almonds*
*100 g/4 oz chopped almonds*
*25 g/1 oz sultanas*
*100 g/4 oz butter* **or** *margarine*
*100 g/4 oz caster sugar*
*30 ml/2 tbsp double cream*
*100 g/4 oz plain* **or** *couverture*
*chocolate*

Line three or four baking sheets
with oiled greaseproof paper. Set
the oven at 180°C/350°F/gas 4.

In a bowl, mix the cherries and
mixed peel with the flaked and
chopped almonds and the sultanas.
Melt the butter or margarine in a
small saucepan, add the sugar and
boil for 1 minute. Remove from the
heat and stir in the fruit and nuts.
Whip the cream in a separate bowl,
then fold it in.

Place small spoonfuls of the
mixture on the prepared baking
sheets, leaving room for spreading.
Bake for 8–10 minutes. After the
biscuits have been cooking for
about 5 minutes, neaten the edges
by drawing them together with a
plain biscuit cutter. Leave the
cooked biscuits on the baking
sheets to firm up slightly before
transferring to a wire rack to cool
completely.

To finish, melt the chocolate in
a bowl over hot water and use to
coat the flat underside of each
biscuit. Mark into wavy lines with a
fork as the chocolate cools.

MAKES 20–24

## ICED PETITS FOURS

*fat for greasing*
*75 g/3 oz plain flour*
*2.5 ml/½ tsp salt*
*50 g/2 oz clarified butter or margarine*
*3 eggs*
*75 g/3 oz caster sugar*

Filling
*jam, lemon curd or buttercream,*
*using 50 g/2 oz butter*

Icing and Decoration
*Glacé icing (page 33, omit chocolate*
*if preferred)*
*food colouring*
*crystallized violets*
*silver balls*
*glacé fruits*
*angelica*
*chopped nuts*

Line and grease a 25 × 15 cm/10 × 6 inch rectangular cake tin. Set the oven at 180°C/350°F/gas 4.

Sift the flour and salt into a bowl and put in a warm place. Melt the clarified butter or margarine without letting it get hot. Put to one side.

Whisk the eggs lightly in a mixing bowl. Add the sugar and place the bowl over a saucepan of hot water. Whisk for 10–15 minutes until thick. Take care that the bottom of the bowl does not touch the water. Remove from the heat and continue whisking until at blood-heat. The melted butter should be at the same temperature.

Sift half the flour over the eggs, then pour in half the melted butter or margarine in a thin stream. Fold in gently. Repeat, using the remaining flour and fat. Spoon gently into the prepared tin and bake for 30–40 minutes. Cool on a wire rack.

Cut the cold cake in half horizontally, spread with the chosen filling and sandwich together again. Cut the cake into small rounds, triangles or squares and place on a wire rack set over a large dish. Brush away loose crumbs.

Make up the icing to a coating consistency which will flow easily. Tint part of it with food colouring, if wished. Using a small spoon, coat the top and sides of the cakes with the icing or, if preferred, pour it over the cakes, making sure that the sides are coated evenly all over. Place the decorations on top and leave to set.

MAKES 18–24

## WINTER TEA

*a selection of sandwiches
filled with:
cream cheese and cucumber
ham, asparagus and mustard
butter
beef and horseradish
sardine and freshly chopped
chives*

*muffins and crumpets served
with preserves, marmite and
anchovy paste*

*rich gingerbread
Dundee cake
corkers
shortbread
macaroons*

*Assam
Earl Grey*

## BROWNIES

*fat for greasing
150 g/5 oz margarine
150 g/5 oz caster sugar
2 eggs
50 g/2 oz plain flour
30 ml/2 tbsp cocoa powder
100 g/4 oz walnuts, chopped*

Line and grease a shallow 15 cm/
6 inch square tin. Set the oven at
180°C/350°F/gas 4.

Cream the margarine and sugar
in a mixing bowl until light and
fluffy. Beat in the eggs. Sift the
flour and cocoa powder into a
second bowl, then fold in. Add half
the chopped walnuts to the
mixture.

Spread the mixture evenly in the
prepared tin and bake for 10
minutes; then sprinkle the rest of
the walnuts all over the surface.
Bake for 15 minutes more. Cool in
the tin. When cold, cut into
equal squares.

MAKES ABOUT 9

## AFTERNOON TEA
## AND HIGH TEA

Afternoon tea was originally known as low tea, since it was taken in low armchairs, as opposed to high tea that was, and still is, eaten while seated around the dining-table. Low tea was an aristocratic and upper middle-class ritual – a time for exchanging gossip, catching up on news of the latest fashions, a chance to meet with one's friends in an elegant, refined, drawing-room atmosphere, to drink tea from the best china or porcelain and nibble dainty sandwiches and pastries. It was usually taken at 4 o'clock and was followed by dinner at 8 or 9 in the evening. High tea, on the other hand, was a much more mundane meal  it was the hard-earned meal that workers craved as they returned home from long, hard hours in mines, factories, mills, foundries and shops. It was eaten as soon as the workers arrived home at 5.30 or 6 o'clock, and all the family tucked into cold meats, pies, bread, cheese and pickles, substantial cakes and numerous cups of tea. It was the last meal of the day, followed only by a hot drink and perhaps a biscuit or sandwich later in the evening.

## MRS BEETON'S
## JAM TARTLETS

*puff pastry trimmings (page 44)*
*flour for rolling out*
*jam* **or** *marmalade*

Set the oven at 200 °C/400°F/gas 6. Roll out the pastry to about 5 mm/¼ inch thickness on a lightly floured surface and use it to line 7.5 cm/3 inch patty tins or foil tartlet cases. Bake blind for 7–10 minutes. Turn off the heat and dry the empty cases in the oven for another 3–4 minutes. Cool, then fill with jam or marmalade.

# $\mathscr{B}$ISCUITS

*These recipes make delicious nibbles to have with tea or coffee at any time of the day. Make them in advance and store carefully in air-tight tins.*

## SHORTBREAD

*fat for greasing*
*100 g/4 oz plain flour*
*1.25 ml/¼ tsp salt*
*50 g/2 oz rice flour, ground rice **or** semolina*
*50 g/2 oz caster sugar*
*100 g/4 oz butter*

Invert a baking sheet, then grease the surface now uppermost. Set the oven at 180°C/350°F/gas 4.

Mix all the ingredients in a mixing bowl. Rubb in the butter until the mixture binds together to a dough. Shape into a large round about 1 cm/½ inch thick. Pinch up the edges to decorate. Place on the prepared baking sheet, and prick with a fork. Bake for 40–45 minutes. Cut into wedges while still warm.

MAKES 8 WEDGES

## FLAPJACKS

*fat for greasing*
*50 g/2 oz margarine*
*50 g/2 oz soft light brown sugar*
*30 ml/2 tbsp golden syrup*
*100 g/4 oz rolled oats*

Grease a 28 × 18 cm/11 × 7 inch baking tin. Set the oven at 160°C/325°F/gas 3. Melt the margarine in a large saucepan. Add the sugar and syrup, and warm gently. Do not boil. Remove from the heat and stir in the oats.

Press into the prepared tin, then bake for 25 minutes or until firm. Cut into fingers while still warm and leave in the tin to cool.

MAKES ABOUT 20

## CHOCOLATE CHIP COOKIES

*fat for greasing*
*150 g/5 oz plain flour*
*1.25 ml/¼ tsp salt*
*2.5 ml/½ tsp bicarbonate of soda*
*100 g/4 oz butter or margarine*
*50 g/2 oz caster sugar*
*50 g/2 oz soft light brown sugar*
*1 egg, beaten*
*2.5 ml/½ tsp vanilla essence*
*75 g/3 oz chocolate chips*

Thoroughly grease two or three baking sheets. Set the oven at 180°C/350°F/gas 4.

Mix the flour, salt and bicarbonate of soda in a bowl.

Beat the butter or margarine until soft, add the sugars and beat until light and fluffy. Beat in the egg and vanilla essence. Stir in the flour and chocolate chips.

Scoop up a teaspoonful of the dough. Use a second teaspoon to transfer the dough to the prepared baking sheets. Repeat, spacing about 5 cm/2 inches apart.

Bake for 10–12 minutes, until golden. Leave to stand for 5 minutes, then cool on a wire rack.

MAKES 26–30

## ALMOND MACAROONS

*fat for greasing*
*2 egg whites*
*150 g/5 oz caster sugar*
*100 g/4 oz ground almonds*
*10 ml/2 tsp ground rice*
*split almonds or halved glacé cherries*

Grease two baking sheets and cover with rice paper. Set the oven at 160°C/325°F/gas 3.

In a clean dry bowl, whisk the egg whites until frothy but not stiff enough to form peaks. Stir in the sugar, ground almonds, and ground rice. Beat with a wooden spoon until thick and white.

Put small spoonfuls of the mixture 5 cm/2 inches apart on the prepared baking sheets or pipe them on. Place a split almond or halved glacé cherry on each macaroon and bake for 20 minutes or until pale fawn in colour. Cool slightly on the baking sheets, then finish cooling on wire racks.

MAKES ABOUT 10

# HIGH TEA

*This is a real family affair. A hearty, filling meal of hot or cold savouries, breads, cheeses, pickles, jam and cakes is perfect for children coming home from school or as a family meal at weekends.*

## WELSH RAREBIT

*25 g/1 oz butter* **or** *margarine*
*15 ml/1 tbsp plain flour*
*75 ml/3 fl oz milk* **or** *45 ml/3 tbsp milk and*
*30 ml/2 tbsp ale* **or** *beer*
*5 ml/1 tsp French mustard*
*a few drops Worcestershire sauce*
*100–150 g/4–5 oz Cheddar cheese, grated*
*salt and pepper*
*4 slices bread*
*butter for spreading*

Melt the fat in a saucepan over gentle heat, and stir in the flour. Cook together for 2–3 minutes, stirring all the time; do not let the flour colour. Stir in the milk and blend to a smooth, thick mixture; then stir in the ale or beer, if used, the mustard and Worcestershire sauce. Add the cheese gradually, stir in, and season to taste. Remove from the heat as soon as the mixture is well blended.

Remove the crusts from the bread and toast lightly on both sides. Butter one side well and spread the cheese mixture on the buttered sides. Grill briefly, if liked, using high heat, to brown the surface of the cheese mixture. Serve immediately.

SERVES 4

# TRADITIONAL CORNISH PASTIES

Pastry
*500 g/18 oz plain flour*
*5 ml/1 tsp salt*
*150 g/5 oz lard*
*60 ml/4 tbsp shredded suet*
*cold water*
*flour for rolling out*
*beaten egg for glazing*

Filling
*1 large **or** 2 small potatoes*
*1 small turnip*
*1 onion*
*salt and pepper*
*300 g/11 oz lean chuck steak, finely chopped*

Set the oven at 230°C/450°F/gas 8.

Make the pastry first. Sift the flour and salt together in a mixing bowl. Rub in the lard, and mix in the suet. Moisten with enough cold water to make a stiff dough. Roll out on a lightly floured surface, and cut into eight 15 cm/6 inch rounds.

Slice all the vegetables thinly, mix together, and season well. Divide between the pastry rounds, placing a line of mixture across the centre of each round. Place equal amounts of the chopped meat on top of the vegetables.

Dampen the pastry edges of each round. Lift them to meet over the filling. Pinch together to seal, and flute the edges. Make small slits with a sharp knife in both sides of each pasty near the top. Mark one end of each pasty with the initial of the person who will eat it, either by making small slits, or by pinching up the pastry with thumb and forefinger in the shape of the initial.

Place the pasties on a baking sheet, and brush with beaten egg. Bake for 10 minutes, then reduce the temperature to 180°C/350°F/gas 4, and bake for a further 45 minutes, or until the meat is tender when pierced by a thin, heated skewer through the top of a pasty. Serve hot or cold.

MAKES 8

## SCOTCH EGGS

*250 g/9 oz sausagemeat*
*15 ml/1 tbsp plain flour*
*1 egg*
*10 ml/2 tsp water*
*salt and pepper*
*4 hard-boiled eggs*
*50 g/2 oz soft white breadcrumbs*
*oil for deep drying*
*parsley sprigs to garnish*

Divide the sausagemeat into four equal pieces. On a lightly floured surface, roll each piece into a circle 13 cm/5 inches in diameter. Beat the egg with the water. Season the remaining flour with salt and pepper and toss the hard-boiled eggs in it.

Place an egg in the centre of each circle of sausagemeat and mould evenly round the egg, making sure it fits closely. Seal the joins with the beaten egg and pinch well together. Mould into a good shape, brush all over with beaten egg, and then roll it in the breadcrumbs, covering the surface evenly.

Put enough oil to cover the Scotch eggs into a deep pan and heat it to 170°C/340°F. Fry the Scotch eggs for 5–6 minutes until golden brown. Drain the Scotch eggs on absorbent kitchen paper. Cut in half lengthways and garnish each half with a small parsley sprig.

Serve hot with Fresh Tomato Sauce (page 42) or cold with a crisp salad.

SERVES 4

## FRESH TOMATO SAUCE

*30 ml/2 tbsp olive oil*
*1 onion, finely chopped*
*1 garlic clove, crushed (optional)*
*1 rasher streaky bacon, without rinds, chopped*
*800 g/1¾ lb tomatoes, peeled and chopped*
*salt and pepper*
*a pinch of sugar*

Heat the oil in a saucepan, and fry the onion, garlic, and bacon over gentle heat for 5 minutes. Add the remaining ingredients, cover, and simmer gently for 30 minutes.

Purée until smooth. Reheat and re-season if required.

MAKES ABOUT
500 ml/17 fl oz

## POTTED SHRIMPS
## OR PRAWNS

*200 g/7 oz unsalted butter*
*400 g/14 oz cooked, peeled shrimps* **or**
*prawns*
*1.25 ml/¼ tsp ground white pepper*
*1.25 ml/¼ tsp ground mace*
*1.25 ml/¼ tsp ground cloves*
*melted clarified butter*

Melt the butter in a saucepan and heat the shellfish very gently, without boiling, with the pepper, mace and cloves. Turn into small pots with a little of the butter. Leave the remaining butter until the residue has settled, then pour the butter over the shellfish.

Chill until firm, then cover with clarified butter. To prepare this, put some butter in a saucepan, heat it gently until it melts, then continue to heat slowly without browning, until all bubbling ceases (this shows the water has evaporated). Remove from the heat and skin off any scum that has risen to the top. Let it stand for a few minutes for any sediment to settle, then gently pour the clear butter into a basin or jar, leaving the sediment behind. If there is a lot of sediment, it may be necessary to strain the fat through a fine sieve or piece of muslin.

Store in a refrigerator for not more than 48 hours before use.

MAKES ABOUT 500 g/18 oz

### SUMMER TEA

*dainty sandwiches filled with:*
*smoked salmon and cream cheese*
*cucumber*
*pâté de foie gras and watercress*
*egg mayonnaise with mustard and cress*

*rich scones with preserves and clotted cream*

*Victoria sandwich*
*florentines*
*eclairs*
*iced and chocolate petits fours*
*brandy snaps*

*Lapsang souchong*
*Darjeeling*
*iced coffee*

## VEAL AND HAM PIE

*½ quantity puff pastry (page 44)*
*500 g/18 oz veal*
*250 g/9 oz ham*
*salt*
*2.5 ml/½ tsp pepper*
*2.5 ml/½ tsp mixed herbs*
*2.5 ml/½ tsp ground mace*
*grated rind of 1 lemon*
*well-flavoured, cooled and jellied stock*
*2 hard-boiled eggs, sliced*
*flour for rolling out*
*beaten egg for glazing*

Set the oven at 220°C/425°F/gas 7.

Prepare the pastry and leave in a cool place until required.

For quality, choose fillet of veal; for economy, use breast or neck. Cut the veal and ham into 1 cm/½ inch cubes, and add the seasonings and flavourings. Heat the stock until melted and mix a small amount in with the meat. Put half the meat mixture into a 500 ml/ 17 fl oz pie dish, cover with the sliced eggs and add the remaining meat mixture. Moisten with the stock but do not allow the liquid to cover the meat mixture completely.

Roll out the pastry on a lightly floured surface to about 5 mm/¼ inch thick, and cut it to fit the top of the pie dish. Dampen the edge of the dish with water. Use some of the trimmings to line the rim of the dish. Dampen the pastry rim, lift the top crust into position, and pinch together to seal the edge. Make a hole in the centre of the crust with a skewer to allow the steam to escape, garnish with pastry leaves, and brush with beaten egg. Bake for 15 minutes, then reduce the temperature to 180°C/350°F/gas 4, and bake for 1½ hours.

Remove the pie from the oven, make a second hole in the crust and carefully pour in a little more melted stock. Leave to cool thoroughly, preferably overnight.

Serve cold with salads.

SERVES 6 – 8

## PUFF PASTRY

*200 g/7 oz plain flour*
*1.25 ml/¼ tsp salt*
*200 g/7 oz butter*
*2.5 ml/½ tsp lemon juice*
*about 100 ml/4 fl oz cold water*
*flour for rolling out*

Sift together the flour and salt into

a bowl and rub in 50 g/2 oz of the butter. Add the lemon juice to the flour and mix to a smooth dough with cold water. Shape the remaining butter into a rectangle on greaseproof paper.

Roll out the dough on a lightly floured surface into a strip a little wider than the butter and rather more than twice its length. Place the butter on one half of the pastry, fold the other half over it, and press the edges together with the rolling pin. Leave in a cool place for 15 minutes to harden the butter.

Roll out the dough into a long strip. Fold the bottom third up and the top third down, press the edges together with the rolling pin, and turn the pastry so that the folded edges are on the right and left. Roll and fold again, cover, and leave in a cool place for 15 minutes. Repeat this process until the pastry has been rolled out six times. Finally, roll out as required and leave to cool for 20 minutes before baking.

MAKES ABOUT 500 g/18 oz

## PLUM BREAD

*100 g/4 oz prunes*
*fat for greasing*
*100 g/4 oz butter*
*100 g/4 oz soft light brown sugar*
*2.5 ml/½ tsp ground mixed spice*
*2.5 ml/½ tsp ground cinnamon*
*2.5 ml/½ tsp gravy browning*
*2 eggs*
*15 ml/1 tbsp brandy*
*100 g/4 oz sultanas*
*100 g/4 oz currants*
*175 g/6 oz self-raising flour*
*a pinch of salt*

Soak the prunes overnight in cold water. Drain well and pat dry. De-stone and chop the prunes finely.

Set the oven at 140°C/275°F/gas 1. Line and grease a 23 × 13 × 7 cm/9 × 5 × 3 inch loaf tin.

Cream the butter and sugar in a large bowl until light and fluffy, then beat in the spices and gravy browning. Beat the eggs lightly in a bowl, mix with the brandy, and beat. Toss all dried fruit in a little of the flour. Mix the remaining flour with the salt, and fold in; then fold in all the dried fruit. Turn the mixture into the prepared tin and level the top. Bake for 3 hours.

# $\mathscr{O}$THER DRINKS

*For those who are not fond of tea, or as a change, serve
some of these refreshing drinks. Iced fruit juices are perfect
for a summer tea, and children will love the milk shakes at
any time of the year.*

## ICED COFFEE (1)

*250 ml/8 fl oz strong black coffee
50 g/2 oz sugar
500 ml/17 fl oz milk
a few drops vanilla essence
100 ml/4 fl oz single cream
ice cubes
60 ml/4 tbsp ice cream (optional)*

Mix the coffee with the sugar in a
jug, and stir until it has dissolved.
Add the milk and vanilla essence.
Chill thoroughly, and stir in the
cream gently.

Fill 4–6 large glasses a quarter full
with ice cubes, pour the coffee over
them, and top with a spoonful of
ice cream, if liked.

SERVES 4–6

### Iced Coffee (2)

*45 ml/3 tbsp coffee essence
750 ml/1¼ pints chilled milk
100 ml/4 fl oz double cream, lightly
whipped
1.25 ml/¼ tsp ground cinnamon*

Blend the coffee essence into the
milk in a jug, and pour into 4–6
large glasses. Top each glass with a
spoonful of cream, and sprinkle
with the cinnamon.

SERVES 4–6

## BASIC MILK SHAKE

*1 litre/1¾ pints milk*
*40 ml/8 tsp concentrated fruit juice* **or**
*fruit syrup*
*4 scoops ice cream, suited to the fruit*
*flavour used*

Either simply stir the chosen flavouring into the milk, chill, and add the ice cream just before serving; or, mix all the ingredients together and chill well. Then just before serving, whisk thoroughly, or process briefly in a blender. Serve while still frothy.

For a coffee milk shake, substitute coffee essence for the fruit flavouring. Use vanilla, chocolate or coffee ice cream.

For a ginger milk shake, use ginger syrup from a jar of stem ginger instead of fruit juice. Add 10 ml/2 tsp finely chopped stem ginger to the other ingredients when mixing.

SERVES 4

## LEMONADE

*pared rind and juice of 4 large lemons*
*20 ml/4 tsp white sugar*
*1 litre/1¾ pints water*

Put the lemon rind and juice in a jug with the sugar. Bring the water to the boil, pour into the jug and stir well. Cover and leave until quite cold; then strain and use.

SERVES 4–6

## ORANGEADE

*pared rind and juice of 4 large oranges*
*white sugar*
*1 litre/1¾ pints water*

Put the orange rind and juice in a jug with sugar to taste; if the orange is very sweet the sugar can be omitted. Bring the water to the boil, pour into the jug and stir well. Cover and leave until quite cold; then strain and use.

SERVES 4–6

# INDEX